Bettendorf Public Library
Information Center
www.bettendorflibrary.com

MW00947534

WITHDRAWN

Ohio Dominican University
Information Center
from the dehumanizer

Pebble® Plus

Sharks

Goblin Shark

by Deborah Nuzzolo

Consulting Editor: Gail Saunders-Smith, PhD

Consultant: Jody Rake, member
Southwest Marine/Aquatic Educators' Association

Capstone press®

Mankato, Minnesota

Pebble Plus is published by Capstone Press,
151 Good Counsel Drive, P.O. Box 669, Mankato, Minnesota 56002.
www.capstonepress.com

Copyright © 2009 by Capstone Press, a Capstone Publishers company. All rights reserved.
No part of this publication may be reproduced in whole or in part, or stored in a retrieval system, or
transmitted in any form or by any means, electronic, mechanical, photocopying, recording, or otherwise,
without written permission of the publisher. For information regarding permission, write to Capstone Press,
151 Good Counsel Drive, P.O. Box 669, Dept. R, Mankato, Minnesota 56002.
Printed in the United States of America

1 2 3 4 5 6 14 13 12 11 10 09

Library of Congress Cataloging-in-Publication Data
Nuzzolo, Deborah.
    Goblin shark / by Deborah Nuzzolo.
    p. cm. — (Pebble plus. Sharks)
    Includes bibliographical references and index.
    ISBN-13: 978-1-4296-2259-2 (hardcover)
    ISBN-10: 1-4296-2259-8 (hardcover)
    1. Goblin shark — Juvenile literature. I. Title. II. Series.
QL638.95.M58N89 2009
597.3'3 — dc22   2008021984

Summary: Simple text and photos describe the goblin shark, where it lives, and what it does.

Editorial Credits
Jenny Marks, editor; Ted Williams, set designer; Kim Brown, book designer; Jo Miller, photo researcher

Photo Credits
Corbis/Reuters/Sea Life Park, cover, 1, 5, 13, 19
Seapics.com, 7, 9, 11, 15, 17, 21

Note to Parents and Teachers

The Sharks set supports national science standards related to the characteristics and behavior of animals. This book describes and illustrates goblin sharks. The images support early readers in understanding the text. The repetition of words and phrases helps early readers learn new words. This book also introduces early readers to subject-specific vocabulary words, which are defined in the Glossary section. Early readers may need assistance to read some words and to use the Table of Contents, Glossary, Read More, Internet Sites, and Index sections of the book.

Table of Contents

v 597.33
UU

Goblin Sharks

What is the strangest shark
in the sea?
It's the goblin shark.
A long head and tail
give it an odd shape.

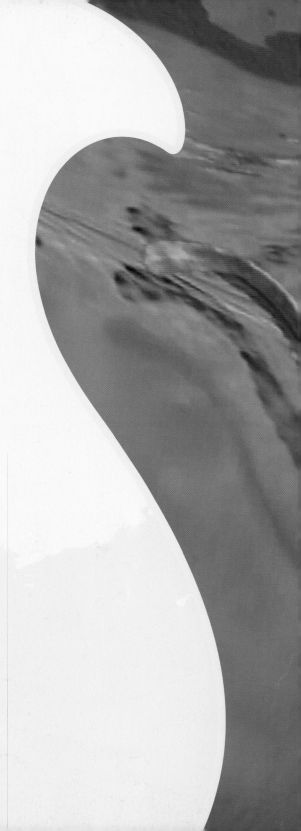

5

Goblin sharks live

in deep water.

They swim

near the ocean floor.

Goblin Shark Pups

No one has ever seen
a goblin shark pup.
Most kinds of shark pups
look just like adults
when they are born.

9

What They Look Like

The goblin shark has
a soft, pink body.

It has small, rounded fins.

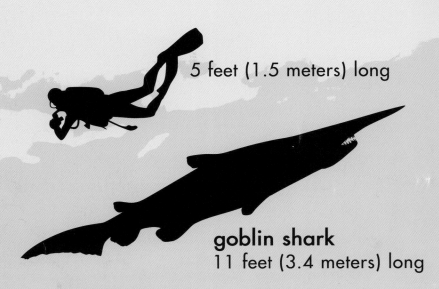

5 feet (1.5 meters) long

goblin shark
11 feet (3.4 meters) long

11

A gobin shark's flat snout
is shaped like a paddle.
From the side,
it looks like
a long, pointed nose.

Hunting

To catch food,

a goblin shark's jaws

reach out

to snap up prey.

The shark's thin, pointed teeth jab prey like a fork.

Goblin sharks eat
fish, squid, and crabs.

People don't need to fear
these deep swimmers.

Glossary

fin — a body part that fish use to swim and steer in water

jab — to poke very quickly

prey — an animal hunted by another animal for food

pup — a young shark

snout — the front part of an animal's head that sticks out

squid — a sea animal with a long, soft body and 10 tentacles

Read More

Crossingham, John, and Bobbie Kalman. *The Life Cycle of a Shark.* The Life Cycle Series. New York: Crabtree, 2006.

Lindeen, Carol K. *Sharks.* Under the Sea. Mankato, Minn.: Capstone Press, 2005.

Thomson, Sarah L. *Amazing Sharks!* An I Can Read Book. New York: HarperCollins, 2005.

Internet Sites

FactHound offers a safe, fun way to find educator-approved Internet sites related to this book.

Here's what to do:

1. Visit *www.facthound.com*

2. Choose your grade level.

3. Begin your seach.

This book's ID number is 9781429622592.

FactHound will fetch the best sites for you!

Index

Word Count: 122
Grade: 1
Early-Intervention Level: 18